Watson

by Iain Gray

LangSyne

PUBLISHING

WRITING *to* REMEMBER

Lang**Syne**

PUBLISHING

WRITING *to* REMEMBER

79 Main Street, Newtongrange,
Midlothian EH22 4NA
Tel: 0131 344 0414   Fax: 0845 075 6085
E-mail: info@lang-syne.co.uk
www.langsyneshop.co.uk

Design by Dorothy Meikle
Printed by Ricoh Print Scotland
© Lang Syne Publishers Ltd 2015

ISBN 978-1-85217-211-4

Watson

MOTTO:
Flourishing Unexpectedly.

Echoes of a far distant past
can still be found in most names

Chapter one:

Origins of Scottish surnames

by George Forbes

It all began with the Normans.

For it was they who introduced surnames into common usage more than a thousand years ago, initially based on the title of their estates, local villages and chateaux in France to distinguish and identify these landholdings, usually acquired at the point of a bloodstained sword.

Such grand descriptions also helped enhance the prestige of these arrogant warlords and generally glorify their lofty positions high above the humble serfs slaving away below in the pecking order who only had single names, often with Biblical connotations as in Pierre and Jacques.

The only descriptive distinctions among this peasantry concerned their occupations, like Pierre the swineherd or Jacques the ferryman.

The Normans themselves were originally Vikings (or Northmen) who raided, colonised and eventually settled down around the French coastline.

They had sailed up the Seine in their long-boats in 900AD under their ferocious leader Rollo and ruled the roost in north east France before sailing over to conquer England, bringing their relatively new tradition of having surnames with them.

It took another hundred years for the Normans to percolate northwards and surnames did not begin to appear in Scotland until the thirteenth century.

These adventurous knights brought an aura of chivalry with them and it was said no damsel of any distinction would marry a man unless he had at least two names.

The family names included that of Scotland's great hero Robert De Brus and his compatriots were warriors from families like the De Morevils, De Umphravils, De Berkelais, De Quincis, De Viponts and De Vaux.

As the knights settled the boundaries of

their vast estates, they took territorial names, as in Hamilton, Moray, Crawford, Cunningham, Dunbar, Ross, Wemyss, Dundas, Galloway, Renfrew, Greenhill, Hazelwood, Sandylands and Church-hill.

Other names, though not with any obvious geographical or topographical features, nevertheless derived from ancient parishes like Douglas, Forbes, Dalyell and Guthrie.

Other surnames were coined in connection with occupations, castles or legendary deeds. Stuart originated in the word steward, a prestigious post which was an integral part of any large medieval household. The same applied to Cooks, Chamberlains, Constables and Porters.

Borders towns and forts – needed in areas like the Debateable Lands which were constantly fought over by feuding local families – had their own distinctive names; and it was often from them that the resident groups took their communal titles, as in the Grahams of Annandale, the Elliots and Armstrongs of the East Marches, the Scotts and Kerrs of Teviotdale and Eskdale.

Even physical attributes crept into surnames, as in Small, Little and More (the latter being 'beg' in Gaelic), Long or Lang, Stark, Stout, Strong or Strang and even Jolly.

Mieklejohns would have had the strength of several men, while Littlejohn was named after the legendary sidekick of Robin Hood.

Colours got into the act with Black, White, Grey, Brown and Green (Red developed into Reid, Ruddy or Ruddiman). Blue was rare and nobody ever wanted to be associated with yellow.

Pompous worthies took the name Wiseman, Goodman and Goodall.

Words intimating the sons of leading figures were soon affiliated into the language as in Johnson, Adamson, Richardson and Thomson, while the Norman equivalent of Fitz (from the French-Latin 'filius' meaning 'son') cropped up in Fitzmaurice and Fitzgerald.

The prefix 'Mac' was 'son of' in Gaelic and clans often originated with occupations – as in MacNab being sons of the Abbot, MacPherson and MacVicar being sons of the minister and MacIntosh being sons of the chief.

The church's influence could be found in the names Kirk, Clerk, Clarke, Bishop, Friar and Monk. Proctor came from a church official, Singer and Sangster from choristers, Gilchrist and Gillies from Christ's servant, Mitchell, Gilmory and Gilmour from servants of St Michael and Mary, Malcolm from a servant of Columba and Gillespie from a bishop's servant.

The rudimentary medical profession was represented by Barber (a trade which also once included dentistry and surgery) as well as Leech or Leitch.

Businessmen produced Merchants, Mercers, Monypennies, Chapmans, Sellers and Scales, while down at the old village watermill the names that cropped up included Miller, Walker and Fuller.

Other self explanatory trades included Coopers, Brands, Barkers, Tanners, Skinners, Brewsters and Brewers, Tailors, Saddlers, Wrights, Cartwrights, Smiths, Harpers, Joiners, Sawyers, Masons and Plumbers.

Even the scenery was utilised as in Craig, Moor, Hill, Glen, Wood and Forrest.

Rank, whether high or low, took its place with Laird, Barron, Knight, Tennant, Farmer, Husband, Granger, Grieve, Shepherd, Shearer and Fletcher.

The hunt and the chase supplied Hunter, Falconer, Fowler, Fox, Forrester, Archer and Spearman.

The renowned medieval historian Froissart, who eulogised about the romantic deeds of chivalry (and who condemned Scotland as being a poverty stricken wasteland), once sniffily dismissed the peasantry of his native France as the jacquerie (or the jacques-without-names) but it was these same humble folk who ended up overthrowing the arrogant aristocracy.

In the olden days, only the blueblooded knights of antiquity were entitled to full, proper names, both Christian and surnames, but with the passing of time and a more egalitarian, less feudal atmosphere, more respectful and worthy titles spread throughout the populace as a whole.

Echoes of a far distant past can still be found in most names and they can be borne with pride in commemoration of past generations who fought and toiled in some capacity or other to make our nation what it now is, for good or ill.

Chapter two:

Flowers of the forest

A diminutive form of the original German forename of Walter, which itself is made up of 'wald', meaning rule, and 'heri', meaning army, Watson simply means 'son of Wat' or 'son of Watt', and variations of spelling in Scotland have included Watsoun, Watsone, and Wattson.

Surnames such as Watt and Walterson, also derived from Walter are, rather confusingly, distinct names in their own right.

A Watson is first recorded in Scotland in 1392, living in Edinburgh, while ten years later, in 1402, a Robert Watsoun is recorded in Aberdeen, while a Sir Donald Watsone appears at Moray in 1493.

Although 'Watson', in its various forms, is found throughout the Scottish Lowlands, it is in the Highlands that much of the romance and drama associated with the name are to be found, through a close kinship with the proud clans of Buchanan and Forbes.

The Buchanans were to be found in western Perthshire and Stirlingshire, while the Forbes clan held sway in the Angus glens and parts of Aberdeenshire and Kincardineshire.

Any Watsons of today who can trace an ancestry back through the centuries to these areas may well be entitled to share in the particular clan's colourful heritage and traditions.

Although regarded as septs, or branches, of both clans, the Watsons are particularly associated with Clan Buchanan, whose proud motto is 'Brighter hence the honour', and crest is a hand holding a tasselled cap.

The present-day Standing Council of Scottish Clans and Chiefs also recognises Watson as being what is officially termed 'a clan unto itself', while a Clan Watson Society displays the motto of 'It has flourished', and the crest of two hands issuing out of the clouds and holding the trunk of an oak tree.

There is also a Watson tartan, designed

in 1935, by the Reverend Mhuir Watson, of Glamis Church, in Angus.

As a sept of Clan Buchanan and Clan Forbes, the Watsons were destined to share in both their fortunes and misfortunes.

Principal branches of Clan Buchanan are Buchanan of that Ilk, of Leng, of Drumakill, of Auchmar, of Arnprior, and of Carbeth, while their progenitor was Anselm, a son of a king of Ulster who found refuge in Scotland from Danish invasions.

It was through helping a grateful Malcolm II of Scotland, who ruled from 1005 to 1034, to repel a similar invasion of Scotland, that he was rewarded with lands to the east of Loch Lomond.

These lands were known in Gaelic as buth chanain, meaning 'canon's seat', and it is from them that the Buchanan name originates.

One colourful member of the clan was John Buchanan of Arnprior, known to posterity as the King of Kippen for his role in a celebrated incident involving James V, who reigned between 1513 and 1542.

The monarch and his boisterous retinue had been enjoying a feast at Stirling Castle when the larder ran empty. Retainers were accordingly despatched into the surrounding countryside, then rich with game, and ordered to kill some deer to restock the royal larder.

Passing Arnprior Castle, however, the fresh kill was promptly purloined by the bold Buchanan.

Informed that the meat was intended for his monarch, Buchanan laughingly replied that if James was King of Scotland, then he, Buchanan, was King of Kippen (Kippen being a local place name).

A contrite Buchanan later had to beg his monarch's forgiveness and, to everyone's amazement, not least Buchanan himself, this was readily granted by the amused monarch.

A rather more tragic incident occurred in September of 1513 when Buchanans and their kinsfolk such as the Watsons were among the 5,000 Scots including James IV, an archbishop, two bishops, eleven earls, fifteen barons, and 300 knights who were killed at the disastrous battle of Flodden.

The battle, remembered in the haunting lament *The Flowers o' the Forest* describing how the cream of Scottish chivalry and manhood was wiped out, was one that should never have been fought in the first place.

The headstrong James IV had embarked on the venture after Queen Anne of France, under the terms of the Auld Alliance between Scotland and her nation, appealed to him to 'break a lance' on her behalf and act as her chosen knight.

The gift of 15,000 French francs may also have acted as an added incentive to the monarch's misplaced sense of chivalry!

Crossing the border into England at the head of a 25,000-strong army that included 7,500 clansmen and their kin, James engaged a 20,000-strong force commanded by the Earl of Surrey.

Despite their numerical superiority and bravery, however, the Scots proved no match for the skilled English artillery and superior military tactics of Surrey.

Nearly thirty-five years later, in 1547, Buchanans and their kinsmen such as the Watsons also fought and died for their nation at the equally disastrous battle of Pinkie, near Musselburgh, on Scotland's east coast, following the invasion of a 25,000-strong English army under the Duke of Somerset.

The Buchanans were among the 3,000 clansmen who fought under the leadership of the Earl of Argyll and who were either killed on the battlefield or were forced to flee to safety.

The battle of Pinkie had been fought during the minority of the infant Mary, Queen of Scots, a monarch for whom the Buchanans and their kinsfolk would once again lay down their lives, this time at the battle of Langside, fought on the southern outskirts of Glasgow in May of 1568.

The battle ended in a resounding defeat of the forces loyal to the ill-starred Queen and her flight into subsequent execution nineteen years later in the Great Hall of Fotheringay Castle, in Northamptonshire.

While Watsons settled in the west of

Scotland forged a kinship with Clan Buchanan, their namesakes in the northeast were kindred of the powerful Clan Forbes.

An antlered stag is the crest and 'Grace me guide' is the motto of this clan that took their name from territory they held in Aberdeenshire.

A John de Forbes is recorded during the reign from 1214 to 1249 of Alexander II, and it was his grandson who was killed defending the strategically vital stronghold of Urquhart Castle, on the shores of Loch Ness, during the bitter and bloody Wars of Independence with England.

An Alexander Forbes was created Lord Forbes in 1442 in gratitude for his services in maintaining the royal authority and rule of law in the northeast, while main branches of the family were Forbes of Culloden, of Pitsligo, Waterton, and Foveran.

A Forbes of Culloden, Duncan by name, was destined to play what transpired to be a tragic role in the Jacobite Rising of 1745.

Chapter three:

Crown and Covenant

It was on August 19, 1745, that Prince Charles Edward Stuart, dubbed by his Hanoverian enemies as the Young Pretender, raised the Standard of the Royal House of the deposed House of Stuart at Glenfinnan after having landed from France on the Hebridean island of Eriskay less than a month before.

Duncan Forbes of Culloden, a skilled lawyer who held the influential post in Scotland of President of the Court of Session, was at heart sympathetic to the Jacobite cause, but with an almost prophetic eye he foresaw the tragic outcome of the attempt to depose the powerful forces of Hanoverian authority.

He attempted in vain to dissuade clan chiefs from rallying to the Prince's cause, and his worst fears were realised when the Rising was finally crushed in the carnage of the battle of Culloden, fought on Drummossie Moor,

near Inverness, on April 16, 1746. Savage
reprisals were carried out against the local
population and even further afield in the grim
aftermath of the battle by the victorious forces
of the Duke of Cumberland, who earned
himself the reviled sobriquet of 'Butcher'
Cumberland.

Forbes attempted to use his influence
after the battle to plead with Cumberland to
show mercy towards the wounded and those
taken prisoner, but his plea fell on deaf ears,
with the haughty commander dismissing the
humanitarian Forbes as "that old woman who
spoke to me of humanity."

A number of Watsons appear on the
muster roll of the Jacobite army of 1745-46,
including a John and Thomas Wattson, who
served with Kilmarnock's Horse.

A John Watson, described in the muster
roll as an innkeeper and brewer from Arbroath,
was with the Duke of Perth's Regiment and,
taken prisoner, was tried and sentenced to
penal servitude in the colonies.

Thomas Watson, a merchant from Arbroath was a lieutenant with the 1st Arbroath Company of the Forfarshire (Ogilvy's) Regiment.

Among other Watsons serving in this regiment were Alexander Watson, from Angus, James Watson, a farmer, and Thomas Watson, a merchant from Kirriemuir. An Alexander Watson, from Banff, served with Lord Lewis Gordon's Regiment.

An entire way of life that had existed for centuries in the Highlands was brutally suppressed in the aftermath of the tragedy of Culloden, and many clansmen and their kinsfolk such as the Watsons were forced to seek a new life elsewhere.

Some turned their backs on their native land forever to seek a new life on foreign shores, while others abandoned the mountains and glens for the Lowlands, where other Watsons had already been settled for centuries.

Many of these Lowland Watsons had previously been involved in a conflict equally

as bitter as that between Jacobites and Hanoverians – the struggle between Crown and Covenant.

The historic National Covenant was first signed in the kirkyard of Greyfriars Church, in Edinburgh, on February 28, 1638, with thousands of ordinary folk subscribing to it as copies were circulated throughout the length and breadth of Scotland.

Those who adhered to the Covenant were known as Covenanters, who pledged to uphold the Presbyterian faith in defiance of the king's claim of supremacy in matters of religion.

Many Covenanters, hounded by the merciless authorities, literally took to the hills of south and southwest Scotland to worship at what were known as open-air conventicles.

The Covenanters were brutally suppressed, particularly after they rose in an armed revolt in 1679, achieving victory over government troops at the battle of Drumclog, near the Ayrshire village of Darvel on June 1 of that year: defeat followed only a few weeks later, however, at the battle of Bothwell Brig, in Lanarkshire.

Many Covenanters who were taken after battle or captured after being hunted down in the hills and valleys were summarily executed on the spot, while others had to endure harsh imprisonment.

The records of the times show that among these many prisoners were a number of Watsons, who figure in two particularly notorious episodes.

In May of 1685, during the bloody period known as the Killing Time, 167 captured Covenanters, including five women, were incarcerated in the forbidding fortress of Dunottar Castle, south of Stonehaven, on the Kincardineshire coast.

Thrown into a dark, cramped and fetid cellar with only two windows, the prisoners slowly succumbed to disease and starvation.

A number were removed to a dungeon beneath the cellar, where conditions were even worse: this prompted the heartbroken wives of two of the prisoners to complain to the authorities of how '...they are not only in a starving condition but must inevitably incur a plague or other fearful diseases.'

No sympathy was forthcoming, however, and conditions became even worse, with one pregnant woman being left to die in misery by her captors.

Tried beyond all endurance, twenty-five desperate prisoners managed to escape through one of the cellar's tiny windows and attempted a perilous descent down the steep cliffs on which the castle perched.

Two of them fell to their deaths, including a James Watson, while another James Watson was among seven other prisoners who died because of his brutal treatment.

In a separate incident, a John Watson was among eight men from the Lanarkshire village of Strathaven who drowned along with 201 other prisoners while being transported to Barbados to be sold as slaves after being captured at the battle of Bothwell Brig.

A total of 250 prisoners had been packed

aboard the *Crown of London*, which sailed for the colonies from Leith in November of 1679.

Anchoring off Orkney on December 10, the ship dragged its anchor during a severe storm and foundered on rocks overlooked by cliffs at the Mull of Deerness.

The crew made their escape from the stricken vessel, but not before locking the hatches that held John Watson and his fellow prisoners.

Some managed to escape, but many fell to their deaths as they were forced back by their captors as they attempted to scale the cliffs.

The cruel record of the Covenanting times also includes the fate of a Thomas Watson, who was killed at the battle of Airds Moss, in Ayrshire, in July of 1680, along with his fiery and charismatic leader Richard Cameron.

Chapter four:

On the world stage

While many bearers of the proud name of Watson played a role in the divisive and destructive conflicts that wracked Scotland for centuries, others have achieved fame and celebrity in rather more constructive pursuits.

In the world of art, George Watson, who was born on his father's estate in Berwickshire in 1767, was the distinguished portrait painter who became the first president of the prestigious Royal Scottish Academy.

Another George Watson, born in Edinburgh in 1654, used some of the vast fortune he accrued as a merchant banker to endow the hospital for children in Edinburgh that, in 1870, became George Watson's College, recognised today as a centre of academic excellence.

Watsons have also played a leading role in the world of science, and include Thomas

Watson, born in Salem, Massachusetts, and who worked as an assistant to the inventor Alexander Graham Bell.

His name is recognised as the first word spoken over the telephone, and this occurred when Bell summoned him by aid of his revolutionary new device from an adjoining room by saying "Watson! Come here, I need you!"

In 1883, Watson founded the Fore River Ship and Engine Company that, after being taken over by the Bethlehem Steel Corporation, became one of the biggest ship-yards operating during the Second World War.

Born in Chicago in 1928, James Dewey Watson, along with Francis Crick of Cambridge University's world-renowned Cavendish Laboratory, found 'the secret of life' when they discovered the structure of the DNA molecule in the early 1950s.

Robert Watson-Watt, born in Brechin, in Scotland, in 1892 and who was descended from the great Scottish inventor James Watt, also contributed to the world of science through his role in the development of radar, a breakthrough that proved crucial during the dark days of the Second World War in the detection and location of enemy aircraft.

In the sporting arena, and a regular visitor over the years to the top golf courses of Scotland, Thomas Sturges Watson is better known as the popular golfer Tom Watson.

Born in Kansas City, Missouri, in 1949, Watson took up his golf career in 1971 after taking a degree in psychology. Winner of the British Open at Turnberry, Ayrshire, in 1977, he won the U.S. Open in 1982.

A highly respected sportsman, he is also an honorary member of Scotland's Royal and Ancient Golf Club of St. Andrews.

In the medical world, albeit a fictional one, Dr. Watson has achieved international fame as the trusty sidekick of Sir Arthur Conan Doyle's cerebral sleuth Sherlock Holmes, whose exploits were originally published in *The Strand Magazine* between 1891 and 1927.

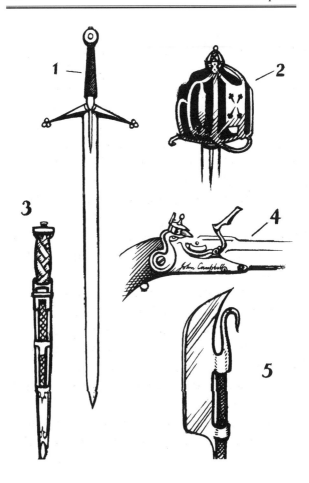

Clan weapons

1)   The claymore or two-handed sword
             (fifteenth or early sixteenth century)

2)   Basket hilt of broadsword
             made in Stirling, 1716

3)   Highland dirk
             (eighteenth century)

4)   Steel pistol *(detail)* made in Doune

5)   Head of Lochaber Axe as carried
             in the '45 and earlier